CHIAROSCURO
Poems in the Dark

Threza Christina Rocque da Motta

CHIAROSCURO
Poems in the Dark

Ibis Libris
Rio de Janeiro
2002

IBIS LIBRIS BOOKS
Published by Ibis Libris Editores
Copyright © Thereza Christina Rocque da Motta, 2002
All rights reserved

First edition

ISBN 85-901613-6-6

Printed in Brazil

Cover: Jorge Jabour Mauad, architect
Electronic Design: Carlos Rocque da Motta, engineer
Photograph: Löis Lancaster

Most of this book was written during e-mail exchanges over the Apollo Poetry list on the Internet.

Ibis Libris Editores
Rua Real Grandeza, 278 / 604
22281-031 Rio de Janeiro – RJ – Brazil

ibislibris@yahoo.com.
tmotta@uol.com.br

To Karl

Contents

TWO E-MAILS FROM DOMINIC, 9

Potomac Blues, 17
Unsinkable ship, 18
Porcelain Princesses, 19
On virtue, 20
Dress my words, 21
When Goddesses decide to mingle, 22
Sans life and sans poème, 24
Love mood, 25
When We Met, 26
Within my heart there is you, 27
Long days into the abyss, 28
Another paradise, 29
You and I, 30
A thousand bells, 31
Men and other causes, 32
Blameless bird, 33
What love should be, 34
Yes, 35
I am what I have been, 36
Away from heaven, 37
Night's Fear, 38
I endlessly weave a carpet of waiting, 39
Thumping hearts, 40
Age 15, 41
Distant island, 42
No Solitude, 43
The wind answered, 44
Sand dimes, 45
Roses back, 46
Because of the darkness of the air, 47
Remember me, 48

Love has sweet bindings, 49
Hang ten, 50
Oblivion, 51
There lies Santorini, 52
Where eternity lies, 53
Thirst, 54
Evergreen, 55
Breathing, 56
Wedding, 57
Simple, 58
Eternity, 59
For all memory, 60
Day, 61
Wandering souls, 62
Soul mating, 63
Landscape at Newport, 64
Walk in my dream, 65
Wild reality, 66
Première in February, 67
007, 68
Torn landscape, 69
Your reflection, 70
Grieves, 71
Flamingo View, 72
While my guitar gently weeps, 73
What I am, 74
COMMENTS, 77

TWO E-MAILS FROM DOMINIC

I

I see the poet as one who makes things new. You are always inspiring to me as well, Thereza. Of all my friends in books, none are as inspiring as you are, because you are doing what many poets of the past wrote about - you are living life's surprises. We always expect from our friends to hear something or read something that freshens our perseverance in living earnestly.

"A thousand bells" is a nice poem. I like it very much. Although I do not understand its full meaning I can guess at its inmost thought.

I like how you arranged your lines in your poem. When you ask this question:

Why do I nest my love
if I would only scatter my wishes
over infinite ponds?

I think that you are digging deep into the true questions people in love often ask themselves - why do I do this? why? And I am sure that you know that as love matures the question becomes less important than the act of loving.

When you say in the last line that

No time can make me turn around

the question is are you walking forward or away from...?

When the heart is overflowing with a beautiful thought we

could write a lovely poem. When the heart is overwhelmed by thoughts that hurt we pour out our story with sorrow.

I love your poem, Thereza. I think that it has pain in it, but I like how you approached the hurt.

II

I read this note you posted below. Your use of the American- English language (my apologies to Tony down under, I guess it would be called Aussie-English there) is so good, even better than that of many Americans. I feel half-ashamed to comment, my own use of English appears so contrived.

I especially liked your term "Leggo language." That is really neat! So descriptive!

Another comment I wanted to make but kept letting slip past is your manner of building a poem in a logical way as well as retaining the lyrical qualities. I think that is very important in Twenty-first century poetry. Poetry is not prose and so many of today's poets, especially new poets, mistake writing the poem as though it were a logical extension of a prose form.

You do not do that, Theresa. You always manage to keep that delicate balance between the poem and the form. I am only sorry that I cannot read your work in the original Portuguese.

In the US we would call the form you use for the Pandora series prose poems. I believe you probably know that. Your critical objectivity toward your own poems seems developed. Your poems do not strain credulity: from what I can tell, you balance the thought with an appropriate sense of value in the subjective and the reader approaches your work with that believability. This is most important in any poem.

Do we ask ourselves, as far as we allow the reader to understand, whether or not we are telling truth through the poem or masking a pseudologic desire? Has the poet tuned the sense of taste? Is the mood of the poem meant to be restful and the experience pleasant? Or is the mood used to jar the reader into either sense or submission? Many things go into writing a poem, statements by themselves won't make poetry.

I hope that I have made myself understood. It is not only bone and muscle that is needed to write poetry well but heart, too. All else, as Lord Tennyson put it is "murmuring of innumerable bees."

When I returned home after three years of war in Southeast Asia I decided shortly thereafter to become a poet. I don't know why. All I know is that is all I truly wanted to be in my life. I saw so much destruction by good men and evil men alike. I shook my fist in the face of God. I counted the old graves of French Legionaires by the side of the road, and made a place in my heart for the new dead I cradled in my arms. Before young manhood abandoned me I thought that I had no tears left. But I was wrong. The person who is not all tears is no poet.

Write from the heart.

Thereza, please keep sending your work, it encourages all of us to strive for the best in life as well as in poetry.

Dominic Tomassetti

Licht, mehr Licht!
Goethe

In my dream
I am not empty.
Gail Wronsky, "Sor Juana's Last Dream"

CHIAROSCURO
POEMS IN THE DARK

Noite

Apenas dois olhos
No claro-escuro
Penetram o muro
Do mundo em destroços
Véu que não voa, repousa
E arde.
Pedro Lage

Night

Only two eyes
in the dim light
pierce the wall
of a crumbling world -
an unwinged weil rests
and burns.
Pedro Lage

1

Potomac Blues
To my father and mother

October reaches no hands.
No matter what paths I follow
there will be no thread to sew my soul.
There is no other place to go now.
No other humming and muttering
of very low voices.
I can hear them at the end of the corridor.
I sneak in,
an intruder into the realm of sight.
I've been away for too long;
I sit and wait inside.
I dare not say what I've known
for a long time.
Hush.
No time will offer us the same
blossoming cherry trees
waving in the distant Potomac.
I embrace you and you are mine now.
As I stand here by the shore,
time flows like an endless river.

August 16, 2000

2
Unsinkable ship
To Lana

Your heart or mine,
how would I know?
You set me thinking
how I would reach you
now that you are gone.

No tides could bear us.
We could not cross the oceans.
I left you as you left me.
We crumbled our fears in our last embrace.
Low mountains sweeping the sight of nightmares.
I shrug in the dim light of a night made of coal.

Whoever might come to heal me?
I would dare to suit you before
you would dare to meet me.

Unsinkable ship riding ashore.

August 20, 2000

3
Porcelain Princesses

Porcelain princesses
are trustful maidens
dressed in organdy
blazing in the sun.

Porcelain maidens
are lustful dancers
dressed in pink
gliding over the floor.

Porcelain dancers
are beautiful pictures
wrapped in linen
slumbering through the night.

Porcelain women
are translucent lilacs
nested in twilight
glittering their light.

August 19, 2000

4

On virtue

A song fills all the emptiness there is.
My whole life spreads before me
and I watch it turn and roll at my feet.
So empty is the room in the darkness
thrilling in its moist expectancy.
I'm aware of the silence that surrounds me
and faint noises come back to my mind.
I've been here so many times and yet
I had not noticed the picture frames on the piano,
the white panes over the windows.
I glare outside while the rain falls
on the garden.
Green walls circle my dreams.
I've been here all my life.
The piano plays a lonely tune
and I'm silent within.
No emptiness can be filled from outside.
Bookshelves cluttered with books,
walls dressed with old paintings,
in this room the void has been as constant
as waiting full hours,
sitting on Persian carpets,
humming a tune in the empty room.

Rio, August 25, 2000

5

Dress my words

I would need a new compass
to rule my soul
and new words to dress myself.
We wait all winter long
to wrap around our necks,
gloves to hide our hands,
and yet
nothing stirs us more than looks.
The eye is the deceiver
and the believer.
I dress my words
with new sounds.
I undress myself from meaning.
Never meant a word I never said.
Words go barefoot, naked,
showing their faces
and smilingly.
Words are dim, are slim,
and are ready to jump, agile, trim.
I wait for the words to come.
They are here and I know them.
I will take them away
and I'll know
what they are.
They search for the unknown,
try to unveil the undiscovered shield.
I gaze through the mist.
My words are there:
somewhere.

August 28, 2000

When Goddesses decide to mingle
*To Dominic, with love,
a re-reading of your dandelion poem*

*When Goddesses decide to mingle,
they astound men with their daring looks
and make their way freely enough
never bothering to know where they're going.
Goddesses always like to astound men.*

*Certainly, goddesses know how to win men over.
And thus are hungry for more.
All men are but faint losses in their mighty hands
twisted elbows and broken backs.
O if they knew who they were!
Goddesses know how to win men over.*

*We went into the sunroom filled with pillows
and the carpets spread through endless floors.
I crawled into a window seat and glanced at the garden
outside the room. O if we knew how cold it would be!*

*Kissing? Who was the fool who invented kissing?
Any men would know how to kiss if a woman had
not pampered him and taken him into her bed.
Beware those killing kisses.*

*Their voice sounds like the wind
over the dark Mediterranean sea.
Dark and plumb like a lead tomb.*

*She enjoys their youth,
and so do I.*

*I watch her bathing, her long white body
plunging into the pool, swimming around
the edges of forgetfulness. Forgive me as I have
lost my time and my eyes looking at her beautiful body.*

*To a man, goddesses like that are all the same.
To a goddess, men like this are all the same human beings.*

September 5, 2000 - 4:39 a.m.

Sans life and sans poème
To Dom and Marge, with all my thanks

Where has all life gone?
Where Shelley sank with his boat?
My eyes wander over the still waters
and my mind tosses in the air.
More life than life could bear.
More soul than the body could hold.
His locks float on the waves
in the ever-moving flow of living water,
washing his eyes, washing his mind,
dipping it in forgetfulness.
O take me where Shelley is.
I won't mourn him,
just hold him close to my breast,
shed his fears and weep for his dying breath.
He won't die within me.
I'll stay with his poetry,
stay with his flame,
his unbearable loss,
his unchangeable love.

September 6, 2000 - 10:17 a.m.

8

Love mood
To Dominic Tomassetti

Love tickles you
whenever you think of it.
Love bugs you all the way.

All decisions are made
Depending on your love mood
today.

August 5, 2000

When We Met
To Tony Burch, a revival

We never met in daylight.
You did not talk to me the first time we met.
We went unnoticed for such a long time
that we don't know when it really happened.

Once you were alone,
then I had a date.
Next you had a girlfriend
and I felt so ashamed.

What made us miss each other
so often?
You crossed my path and I never knew
who you were.
My friends would not have told me
if I'd never asked.
And I wondered who you were,
what you did
and where you went.

Did you wonder about me?
Did you want to see me again?
Were you hiding from me or was I just
invisible to you?

It never mattered much
cause we never said a word
until I crossed your way
and said hello.

September 14, 2000

10

Within my heart there is you

My heart lies in blue
beyond the rising dawn
resting my head in my arms.

I rest my thoughts in your heart.
Where you have been is where I am.
And the bluer you are
the wider my eyes are open.

There are no sighs, no regrets.

All I pursue is with you.

September 15, 2000 - 1:46 a.m.

11

Long days into the abyss

To Dom, because of his debonair accent
To Tony, because of his Australian flair
To Marge, for her mythological airs
To Dean, for his Greek blueness

Long days into the abyss.
Greek inland and islands.
My paradise lost.
Thessalonick coasts.
Macedonian highlands.
The Corinth Canal.

The hills can no longer hold me.
The Ionic Sea lies before me
and I lose sight of the distance.
The Peloponnesian's straits are far away ribs.
I stand against walls of silence
built in murmur.
Wash your shores and pull your boats
aside.
We'll be here for eternity.
Never mind what I say.

Flowers circled by muddy waters
shallow rivers going around the lands
hold me back in time.

Time rolls back its curtains
and we find ourselves in nowhere land.
My heart is there.

Rio, September 15, 2000 - 03:49 a.m.

Another paradise

for one effulgent interval
another paradise could not exist
and just the all that two create
is everything
R. Dean Ludden

Your enfolding arms hold more
than my body.
Nothingness is an exquisite
stem of an unknown flower.
Eyes cannot meet
and hands cannot touch
and yet we dare to say
whatever is carved in stones
for another eternity.
This is paradise.
A succession of new dawns
rising on firm horizons
circling life wherever we may be.
Lift your face
and look at me
under the morning light.
Another moment cannot pass
until this one is gone.

September 16, 2000

13
You and I

Where pureness lies,
there I am
gliding away my laments
slowing down my pace
trimming flowers and waiting
a book in my hands
an enfolded letter
roses on the piano
and I,
solely awaiting
the humming of birds
opening my ears
your safe embrace
my sated eyes
I, shielded by your boldness
you, resting with me
under the blue light.

September 19, 2000 - 11:24 p.m.

14

A thousand bells

A thousand bells make thunders over me
A thousand wands open a thousand doors
and unwanted fears dash over the sky

Why do I nest my love
if I would only scatter my wishes
over infinite ponds?

A thousand years would pass by
and I would take my shattered feelings
away with me

No time can make me turn round

September 23, 2000

15

Men and other causes

I shall write all verses of men tonight.
I shall endure the highest pain
and let the years drift by and let me
demurred.
I shall write to you all poems I regretted
not writing.
And the softer the words carry me along
I shall strive with your memory
of me.

Rio, September 26, 2000

16

Blameless bird

Blameless bird
so colorful feathers
can only hear its
own singing.

Beautiful bird
will never know
we listened to him
singing.

So colorful
so bright
so distant
bird.

August 24, 2000

17
What love should be

*Love should be a safe path
not an insecure trend.
Love should bring you joy
from the same juicy fruit
you taste.
What we blame is not love.
It is our ignorance of love.*

August 20, 2000

18
Yes

Yes
I beli-EVE
in possibilities too
and that's why
I cross my fingers
and wait for the dawn
glancing at long horizons
without spears in my hands.
Hope is all we need
EVEn when we think
we are hopelessly lost.
I BE-li-EVE
in me.

August 18, 2000

19

I am what I have been

I am what I have been
this might suit me best.
The better off I get, the best I will be.
I never shout or whisper.
Whispers haste feelings in old hearts.
Shouts and twisted elbows
turn the corners of an empty city.
Down there cars pass by
passengers pass by
buses
bikes
thunder lights.
Where have I been?
I am what I have been, I say.
What have I been?
A nutshell, an oyster, a beam.
A sunray, a drop, a snowflake.
I am what I think I am.
I have never been me.
When will I begin to be?

August 17, 2000

20

Away from heaven

*No heavens
no dusk
I'm in pure dismay
all skies are dim
and I am lost*

*No heavens, no dusk
distrust my eyes
I've been caught
between sea and sky*

*Don't let heaven take you
where you don't want to go
Heaven awaits you
and so will you go on*

*Nothing stirs under this pure sky
No clouds can lure me
No one can tell me*

*No heavens, no dusk
can embrace me
Take my time
take me
to nowhere land
with you*

August 4, 2000 - 2:58

Night's Fear

My shadow, a darker me
I need to enlighten.
I imagine myself plunging
a new depth.
My soul rises above
a hidden horizon
as I never fail to brew
this long night.
Sing, my nightingale.
Take my soul and shadow
to the harbor of time.
Lie down with me
and wait till dawn.
Twilight's whiskers
are still there.
Open my black tomb
and take me out.
Light
not fear
is what I might.

August 3, 2000 - 5:48

22

I endlessly weave a carpet of waiting

I endlessly weave a carpet of waiting.
Whoever comes to bid me farewell,
sinks in the shore of forgiveness,
dwells in the heart of secrets,
and plunges into my soul and weeps.

I endlessly wait for hours,
lingering over the landscapes of thought,
knowing I will never be awake
on the moment you return.
I shall stay motionless, speechless,
and thrust in sorrow.
My limbs will stray along rivers of time.

Timeless ticking of slumbering clocks,
thick brightness of moving skies,
I relentlessly long for a moment of love
I never had.

Rio de Janeiro, July 31, 2000

23
Thumping hearts

Thumping hearts
beating tips
Every time I lose you
I sense you
never forget you
forgive you
get you
here.
It doesn't matter.

Rough voices,
sore throats,
rough hands
hearts thumping again.

July 24, 2000

24

Age 15

I was never
happy
at 15.
Wonder why
I felt so lonesome
or so left behind.
I wanted to be
somewhere
I couldn't be
and I didn't know
what this place
would be.
I think at 15
I started being
myself.
Although I didn't
know what
was going to happen
next.
I had my first delusion
when my first boyfriend
dumped me
for another Thereza
who, seven years later,
married him.
Then I found out
how lucky I was
not to be
me.

July 24, 2000

25
Distant island

You are a distant island now.
I've turned my back
and see you disappear in the mist.
I'm not turning round.
I'm not going back.
I wish I had never left.
But as I did,
it's past.

September 28, 2000

No Solitude
To Karl

*Now there is no sadness,
no shivering under the cold wind.
Thoughts blown into the shadow
cast into the deep well.
Voices echo and still the haunting moon
is the only witness besides us.
Who are we in this long embrace?
Now there is no solitude
and we know we have found each other.
We stammer and anxiously kiss again.
The long hustling night shields us
under a damp cloak.
Now there is only me and you.
And no remembrance tonight.*

São Paulo, October 3, 2000

27

The wind answered
To Jean Pierre and Marjorie

A silent ship-dot passes
　a pale blue-green horizon
　　on a sea swept silver clean
　　　and I dream.
　　　　Karl W. Stritter

It is your peace I look for
your sacred heart in mine.
Wind will blow and trees will flutter
staggering legs crossing lands.
I will stray along the benches
lingering in the past.
Hold me close to heaven
where no clouds can be seen.
You will find me over bridges of thought
waiting until dawn can rescue me.

Rio, October 7, 2000

28

Sand dimes

And I turned for home with my treasure,
A disc of hardened sand,
Honoring his glory.
Karl W. Stritter

Take me home
and treasure me
like a non postponed letter
a dime in your back pocket
a grin on a blue face.
Take me home
and soothe me.
Spring will come and cover us
with new flowers and breeze.
Shielding skies, long blown clouds,
we wrestle in a dwelling pan,
opening eyes in the dark,
waving on the crest of night,
as long as time will allow us.
Take me home
and love me.

Rio, October 14, 2000 - 4:06 p.m.

29

Roses back
the wild rose of August
with lips of pink-purple fire
and guarding green thorns
awaits the dawn.
Karl W. Stritter

Bring me back the dawn
bring me the roses, their scent
their alluring petals.
Bring me back to myself
nested in silence
torn to pieces
forgotten and unforgiving.
Bring me the wild flower
that grows far away
and plant it near me
here where I stay.

Rio, October 14, 2000 - 4:18 p.m.

30

Because of the darkness of the air
To Marge

Because of the darkness of the air
I shut my eyes and listened to the glistening leaves
the rustling branches above me
and my mind floated in the moonlight over the damp forest.
Desolated fields spread over horizons
casting a void sound in my head.
Damp soft hands holding my arms.
I could feel their warmth around me.
Time has passed and has taken me with it.

Rio, October 15, 2000 - 1:44 a.m.

31
Remember me

Remember me before I'm gone.
Rest your head on my chest and wait until dawn.
We will still be here after all those years.
Who are we now?
Who we wanted to be?
We shared our lives in relentless paths
moving, coming and going and never knowing
when to stop.
Look at me now.
I've been yours for so much time
and you've never seen me.
Your arms have rooted around me
and can't let me go.
I will be here forever.
Hold me and lean over my breast.
Close your eyes
and let your fears fade away.
Motionless, I stir in silence.
Cool my head, my ears and lips.
Sate me when I'm done.
Never leave me again.

October 21, 2000 - 22h13

Love has sweet bindings

Who have we been before we met?
Who were we alone in the crowd
not cherished and unfulfilled?
Who are we as we can't recognize ourselves?
I have been me and you have been yourself.
You have been lost and me too.
I have tasted all wine and eaten my share of bread.
You have starved in the desert
and longed for the oasis.
I have been saved by kindliness.
You have longed for my embrace
and never told me how much you missed me.
I have prayed to see you,
waited to talk to you,
lingered for immemorial time
in the corridors of long winged alleys.
I turned my face away from hurt
and silenced before death.
You wanted me to come
and never asked for it.
We have been away for such a long time
that we never knew when we stopped suffering.
Time has given us peace again.
Love has sweet bindings
and has shielded us under its armor.
Come and share the shades of these long waited hours.
The ripen fruits are waiting to be crunched
under our teeth.
We were bound to love
and thus we live again.

October 21, 2000 - 23h50

33

Hang ten

Like the solitary surfer
racing a primordial crest
we travel in time suspended
on this celestial sea
Karl W. Stritter

Unbound sea
awesome sights
lightnings over the horizon.
I stray over beaches
and sink my feet in the sand.
Seashells, rocks,
fishes scattered in the air
dive with me in a blue wave.

October 22, 2000 - 2:11 p.m.

34
Oblivion

Cast away all tears,
dream with your past days and joy.
Stretch your hands
and touch me.
All is gone, past now.
You may start dreaming,
again.

October 22, 2000 - 2:33 am

35
There lies Santorini

There lies Santorini
in the mist
floating in dim water
pulling its face towards us
open in the crest of time.
There, where Santorini lies,
the mountains pursue the skies
the velvet clouds arise in the dark
and I wait for the small hours
to shut my doors
and blow the candlelight.
Here we are where Santorini lies.
We are young and still willing
to find new stones on ancient beaches.
The sea surrounds us and quenches
our thirst.
Sail with me and we'll find a home there.

October 23, 2000 - 2:21 am

Where eternity lies

Somewhere between death and dreams
I find eternity.
I lie my head down on the green grass
and smell the sweetness of joy.
I will find eternity in a split moment
when you look at me again and smile.
All my life has been a still moment
as a long aria in a well-known opera.
I will wait for a lifetime for you to come.
There where eternity lies,
there are no fogs or twilights.
A wonderful morning spreads over the skies
and I can sense the ever-lit dawn
while I open my eyes.
This is what I have been waiting for:
a stroll in the park and a glimpse of happiness
in a crystal well.
A pond of light is open before me.
A shade of dust sprinkles the landscape
and the stillness of light brings eternity
to somewhere between death and dreams.

October 29,2000 - 2:56 a.m.

37
Thirst
To Jean-Pierre Barakat

There are poems we read
and keep to us.
Others make us think and write.
When a poem comes
we welcome it
as a morning breeze or a tempest.
Our thirst never ends.

November 14, 2000

38

Evergreen

Yet we wonder
why life has such a grasp
on our feelings.
Why have we such trembling
hands and fearing looks?
No wonder we want more air.
Life is breathing.
Breathing green.

November 25, 2000

39
Breathing

I will bring you the joy
I silently kept inside.
We nourished our feelings with hope
and despair
while we were waiting for so long.
Open the windows of light
let life enter your realms
and tell you your angels are here
and all illusion disappeared.

Yes, the search is over
and faith regained.
While we rebuild ourselves once more
tell me what I lack and want.
I need to feel the breathing of things
to sense myself alive.
Every time I learn a new step.
Every time I'll be born again.

December 3, 2000 - 10:27 a.m.

40
Wedding

Wedding cakes
smiling faces
looking at each other
so much in love
so much in happiness
never described
before.
Only after we will know
how long it takes
to be ourselves.
We learn from fall.
And we teach ourselves
to be new.

November 20, 2000 - 10:15 am

Simple

*Love cannot be new
for we have always been in love.
A new love is like a new tree
blooming from an old seed.
It is the same love.
And yet it looks new.
Love cannot be other
for we have always been the same.
And what we know for love
is born in us.
Love has known us before
we were able to find it.
It made us crawl then walk
and now it can make us fly.*

November 20, 2000 - 10:10 am

Eternity

Eternity is much too long to wait.
Bold eyes see too far.
I want to take you in farther dreams,
cling to me
and travel along.
Eternity is too dear to be wasted.
Our words will lose their sense
in time
for our speechless eyes
take us beyond paradise.
Rest with me and learn to be
at ease.
I long for your life
as I long for mine.
Eternity is my home
and thine.

Rio, December 15, 2000 - 4:34 p.m.

43

For all memory

For all memory
let us be together
until we fall apart
like branches of an old tree.

For all words
lets stay closer
so we can find the ways
to reality.

For all days
lets murmur our thoughts
and prayers and be the only
ones to believe.

No matter how long we live
we'll long for eternity
to be part of us.

December 25, 2000 - 11:37 p.m.

44
Day

sunshine colored hills
hustling the green leaves
bringing them to life

November 25, 2000

45

Wandering souls

Souls will wander
until they find shelter
under a morning breeze
where the trees are hushing
and the sun isn't up yet.

I walk with my soul
in my hand
humming tunes of despair.

Let me not go without my soul.
Nor leave it untamed.
Gather my feelings
and enfold me with your arms
and fears.

Let me be here
with you
alone.

January 3, 2001

46

Soul mating

Everlasting breath
of my soul
seizes me
and makes me
wonder
if we were meant
to be
here
or anywhere
in any time of our lives
- were we preexistent
to know who we are?
Forever
is the answer
to any question
you make.

January 5, 2001 - 11:32 a.m.

Landscape at Newport

My visions subdue
before these great waters
and a bird almost touches
the rim of the waves.
I cast pebbles
at the shore
and I know I am there.
Waves of time
can come and go
and I will be the same.
Why have we lived
all those years?
Never will time give us
the answers.
We will go undaunted
trimming the edges
of time.

Boston, January 25, 2001

Walk in my dream

I listen to you while I sleep.
My dreams can reach you
and I can touch you in my mind.
Wander with me through my dreams.
All thoughts about you open small skies
in my mind.
I descend to your valleys
and sit by a slumbering tree.
I frown to see you
and turn my face away while I smile.
I can see you with the corner of my eyes
as you look at me.
I walk with you up and down my dream.
The night shadows our steps
and I dream of you until dawn.

Salem, January 31, 2001 - 1:13 a.m.

49
Wild reality

Reality is beyond your dreams
- wherever you may look for it.
Reality lies beyond the hills
and we can never see it.
We are happy souls
stumbling through life
indeed
flowing the rhythm of life
increasingly high.
Earth loves us.
And we love it back.
That's why we are here.
And we'll always come
back.

Salem, February 4, 2001 - 12:02 a.m.

50

Première in February
Be mine!
St. Valentine's card wish

The first time I got to New York
it was Xmas.
Saks Fifth Ave. & St. Patrick's Cathedral
were there.
Now the second time is a new rentrée
"Do you have your ticket?"
the lady asks.
"No, m'am."
I ain't got a ticket
but I'm back,
to my second première
on a Valentine's Day.

Arriving in Manhattan, New York,
on the evening of February 14, 2001 at 10:30 p.m.

51
007

I live everytime
a little
bit by bit
slowly
dearly
endearingly.

I live everytime
once more
one more
game in Paradise.

I live as many times
as I am reborn.
Nothing more
nothing less.

Twice as much
as anyone
can get.

June 11, 2001 - 1:23 a.m.

Torn landscape

It was not this view
that I've learned to admire.
It was not this word
the life
the divine notion.

Torn landscape.
By pain, by horror,
by chaos.

By the absurd
of being before
distress
and ail
and not being able
to say anything more
than prayers.

September 12, 2001 - 2:02 a.m.
(translation)

53

Your reflection
To Karl

*You are Adam,
the first man.*

*God imposed His hand
upon your head
and gave you life.*

*You are the first being
the first to love
the first to breathe
the first to see the light.*

*You are the first miracle
and the first to laugh.*

*God gave you fruit
gave you trees
gave you animals
gave you land.*

*God loved you
and gave you the power
to change your life.*

*You are Adam,
the Beloved.*

October 3, 2001 - 9 p.m.

Grieves
To Marge

*My grief is deeper
than the well
of my tears.*

*My longing arms
hold more than
the strongest
sorrow.*

*I can't breathe
this autumn air
doomed with filth
and horror.
Can't look
into my mirrored eyes.*

*Shades of trees
stretch out in twilight.*

*I wrap my thoughts
my wishes
and dreams in thin paper
and leave them still
until winter is gone.*

October 9, 2001 - 2 p.m.

Flamingo View
To Oscar Niemeyer

Always the sea framed
by an open window
between an old horizon
and an antique architecture.
Almandrade

Which architecture has arched your arm,
the needless embrace to all loose forms,
veil upon veil, bidding a long farewell,
the horizon still glancing at your eyes,
the empty frames of your easy trace?

Trace the rhythm on the blank sheet,
your poem made of chalk and dust,
concrete arch of your concrete skill,
steel poet, a warning probe,
where have you left your stern profile?

Nothing surprises you, you are older now.
Your panoramic windows gaze at you:
you come close to your own children.

I am the one who visits and listens to you.
Come and embellish my eyes,
draw your secrets from me
- empty mould of your antique vastness.

Fold your drawing sheet
and keep it.
We shall be, in time,
what we have wished for so long.

November 25, 2001 - 5:15 a.m. (translation)

While my guitar gently weeps
To George Harrison, i.m.

Hold me while I cry.
Never will there be a day like this.
While I stand here and pray,
tears flow down my face.

Tell me he's not gone.
Strawberry Fields are forever.
Those days have long past
but we still turn our eyes to Liverpool.

Let me sing another tune.
There are so many to remember.
If he was here he'd play a song,
newer than before.

We've spent so many years
listening to their songs
that they all seem endless.
Those neverending days where music
made its way and took us to paradise.

No, it won't let me down.
Once and again
he'll be slumbering
under the sunshine
that comes.

December 1, 2001

57
What I am

I am all, total, everything and more.

*No rhymes or certainties,
in all there is of most sanctified
and pure, of meekness and reliance,
of pursuit
and nourishment.*

*We are alive
as we are.*

*April 13, 2001 - 2:43 a.m.
(in Dawn, 2001, translation)*

COMMENTS

I like the last one best of all. Islands and continents as thirsty fountains... leveling from brooks... Signifies to me the need of each of us as individuals to partake of the same substance of refreshment.... that we are incomplete when we are apart, no matter what our strength or significance... and "bathing in the waters of the empty ocean" of another being, and seeking those limits is a heightened expression of vulnerability... subtle, and yet very clear to me...This poem speaks volumes to me.

Now, as to the poems you sent me last night after translating them... They are miniature works of art... capturing the depth and beauty of love and the love act. Your translations are very effective, and I know it is not easy to translate a poem from one language to the other. They are poems that I shall want to read over and over again.

Another fascinating poem (When the Goddesses decide to Mingle), Thereza, in several ways. You have a unique and charming way of looking at things. The metaphor, "swimming around the edges of forgetfulness" is wonderful! I truly enjoyed Dress my words and to me there was triple entendre, intended or not. I refer to the main point, plus the use of metaphor, plus a hint of eroticism, and it all came together for me. A very subtle and skillful poem and I thank you for it. On Potomac Blues: Some nice images in this. Thread to sew the soul is a fascinating metaphor... first I have seen of it.

R. Dean Ludden

I am only sorry that I cannot read Portuguese. Your poetry tends toward the lyrical. You express your feelings, thoughts and the things you see very well.

I like this poem you wrote. There is something-special living in the heart of the poet, don't you think? I believe that too many people miss out on living life to its fullest and just dabble in words.

You are a fascinating poet.

It's interesting how you wrote a poem about Artemisia. It is a wonderful name and very poetic. As to the meaning of your poem I can tell that

you are explaining the lover carrying a silent hurt. Artemisia may like to live again in one of your beautiful poems, Thereza Christina.
On Potomac Blues: I just read your poem "October reaches no hands" just a few minutes ago. This poem is so wonderfully fine in English that it must be very beautiful in Portuguese. A father could have no greater tribute than a poem like this from a daughter.
Each of these poems are very good just as you have written them. I do not think they need any changes in the English. I find it nearly impossible to say which I like best, Muse, Echo, Gallatea or Sybille! Here you are at the top of your form.

Dominic Tomassetti

This is really haunting. I'm anxious to see the rest of the book.
On Unsinkable Ship: This has a misty dark blue feeling that I can almost see.
On Love Mood: I like this. It sounds more natural than the others. The others don't seem unnatural. This just sounds like direct thinking. Wonderful imagery.
On Pandora: I am enjoying these more and more as I read them. I'm not sure whether I'm feeling the women you speak for of the woman that is really myself. They are wonderful.
On Pandora: The tiny snatches say more than a longer work could. They are beautiful breath thoughts of not so mysterious women.
On Odysseus: I love this. You have captured a lot of what is in each of us.
This is so full of beautiful images that I had to read it several times. Each time I saw something that I hadn't seen before. Your poems are always very good but I think this is one of the best.

Marjorie L. Compfort

My heart is still pounding with emotion created by your verses. I can only thank you and continue into poetry in motion... Tell me, out of curiosity, did the words pour in your soul in Portuguese first?

Jean Pierre Barakat

I do love this image of you as a publisher, nobly putting other people's work out into the world - just make sure that you have time to do your own. But of course you do, since you are sending me these amazing things that you have written - which move me immensely, and I think that is the most important thing about poetry. In fact your writing makes me feel immeasurably sad, it is so poignant and full of a kind of unnamed loss.

Thanks so much for the poems. They are so poignant, so moving, so sad - almost unbearable really. You have a very interesting voice, very idiosyncratic, very much yours - which is of course exactly what one wants in a poet.

Marion Halligan

I continue to read you work and wonder at your ability to describe so beautifully. It seems my stuff is but a conversion of thought or experience into words anerd that needs but a simple wordsmith to do that. Yours comes from elsewhere.

Tony Burch

On Pandora: It seems a lot of artists were inspired by Mythology...Veronese, Coreggio and Michelangelo and I think Leonardo da Vinci also did splendid drawings of Leda. I didn't want to go without saying that I think you write in the most flowing liquid style. Beautiful. I could glide in it all day

Lana Crawford

The poet trespasses the frontier of voice and all senses, as someone who refuses to be imprisoned, proposing the nudity of the soul, revealing unsuspected dimensions of reality, where many times the subjective aspects are surpassed by the sphere of objectivity presenting the strong structure of the prosaic composition.

Jerrie Hurd

This is a fantastic poem. So descriptive. I particularly like the last two lines:
We shall be, in time,/ what we have wished for so long.
They say so much. This (Flamingo View) is one of your best poems.
I agree with Marge. This is one of your best poems. I am going to have to go to the library to see if I can find an architecture book with some of Oscar Niemeyer's work.
I thank you. I have learned so much about poetry from you I will be forever in your debt. I love poetry that opens windows for me, and makes me think. The images. The ideas you convey are so well crafted there are times I am in awe of your talent.

Karl Stritter

Thereza Christina Rocque da Motta was born in São Paulo in 1957. Poet, translator, attorney, English teacher, and publisher. Was the chief Brazilian researcher for the Guinness Book, the Book of Records (Editora Três, 1992). Published Relógio de Sol (Sundial), 1980, Papel Arroz (Rice Paper), 1981, Joio & trigo (Tares and Wheat), 1982, Areal (Sands), 1995, Sabbath (1998), Alba (Dawn), Ibis Libris, 2001, and the poster-poem Décima Lua (Tenth Moon), 1983; anthologies: Carne Viva (Live Flesh), erotic poetry, 1984, Anthology of the New Brazilian Poetry (1992), both organized by Olga Savary; Contralamúria (Counterwailing), Casa Pindaíba (1994), Intimidades Transvistas (Transviewed Intimacies), with paintings by Valdir Rocha, Escrituras (1997), Anthology of the Contemporary Brazilian Poetry, Editora Alma Azul, Portugal (2000), organized by Álvaro Alves de Faria, Poemas Cariocas (Poems from Rio), Ibis Libris Editores, Rio (2000), organized by herself and Santa Poesia (Saint Poetry), Casarão Hermê (2001) with over 150 poets. Unreleased books of poems: Odysseus, Pandora's Book, Lilacs, Lazuli, Love and Wings, Poems to Marco Polo, Flamingo View, Just Football - a Team of Poems, Spree, and Dawn (in English). Translated books: Essence and Diamond Heart, by A H. Almaas (Editora Rosa dos Tempos, 1992); Instruments of Night and The Chatham School Affair, by Thomas H. Cook (Ed. Lacerda, 2000), besides poems by Anne Morrow Lindbergh, John Keats, W.B. Yeats and Lord Byron. Lives in Rio, where she takes part of poem readings in bookstores, theaters and cafés. Founded Ibis Libris Editores, her own publishing house, in 2000. She is mentioned in the new revised and updated edition of the Encyclopedia of Brazilian Literature (Global Editora, 2001), by Afrânio Coutinho.

SCOR Gráfica TECCI

Impressão e Acabamento:
Scortecci Gráfica
Telefax: (11) 3815-1177
grafica@scortecci.com.br